CANDOMBLÉ

Dancing for the Gods

_____

MONIQUE JOINER SIEDLAK

Oshun
PUBLICATIONS
oshunpublications.com

Cover Design by MJS

Cover Image by daemon-barzai@depositphotos.com

Published by Oshun Publications

www.oshunpublications.com

Books in the Series

African Spirituality Beliefs and Practices

Hoodoo

Seven African Powers: The Orishas

Cooking for the Orishas

Lucumi: The Ways of Santeria

Voodoo of Louisiana

Haitian Vodou

Orishas of Trinidad

Connecting With Your Ancestors

Blood Magic

The Orishas

Vodun: West Africa's Spiritual Life

Marie Laveau: Life of a Voodoo Queen

Contents

Introduction

The world is much more than all that our limited senses can perceive. There is more to life than air, grass, fire, and even the luxuries that we all desire. With the pain, confusion, and chaos that saturate our world today, it has become more imperative than ever for you to find and hold on to something outside of yourself. Something more significant than you, beings without the limitations of your fleshy abode, who hold the world up in their deft hands and have the authority to break and mend you.

The ancient religion of Candomblé seeks to bridge the gap between humanity and divinity. It aims to bring us to the point of complete awareness of our true selves and the powers we have locked up within us. Candomblé is a mirror that powers spiritual awakening. It teaches and shows that there is more to us than we can ever find by ourselves. It aims to open our eyes to see what great heights we can attain when we become aware of our personal gods. What it means to be in constant communion and fellowship with them. We all have Orixás, beings designated from the beginning of time to hold us up, teach us and walk through life with us. Most of the hurt, sickness, and confusion you might experience on your voyage through life stems from ignorance and obliviousness to these powers.

I have written this book not just as a guide for those in pursuit of a higher purpose and are interested in discovering it through Candomblé but also as a documentation of my journey to identifying my true self and drawing into the powers thereof. Unlike many other organized religions, Candomblé doesn't demand subservience or ask that you be ruled by the fear of punishment or the unknown. As a religion and a movement, its end goal is to show you that you do not have to go through life independently. It aims to teach you that even when humans let you down and leave you groping in the dark, there will constantly be a light to guide you if you only let yourself see, accept and follow it.

I, too, was once in search of something greater. I was once desperately looking for meaning and purpose beyond all of the temporary possessions that the world clings to. I pursued something more permanent and eternal, and I found it in Candomblé. If you, like me, have realized that you need something more than yourself to walk you through the path of life, this is the book for you. In its pages, you will find truths to guide you on your journey and bring you into full knowledge of yourself and your Orixás. As you read, I pray that the hands of Olorun guide your Orixás as they guide you into the pure understanding of the fundamentals of this great path and that in the end; you are reborn into power and peace.

ONE

Candomblé's History

IN THIS CHAPTER, WE WILL ANSWER A FEW BASIC VITAL questions. Specifically, we will learn how and why Brazil has today's religious groups. After that, we will look at how African religions became a part of that. As we explore changes and traditions within Candomblé, remember that some answers are obvious while some aren't as obvious.

Establishing the Beginning

Brazil was discovered by the Portuguese in the early 1500s. They initially named it "True Cross," but because of the abundance of Brazil wood, it was renamed 'Brazil.' There was excitement when Brazil was first discovered. However, since precious metals weren't found at the time, Portugal turned to more lucrative dealings with Asia. Some trade took place with the native Brazilians for wood. Decades after the discovery of Brazil, Portugal developed a renewed interest in trading with the country. As a result, Portugal set up a government in Brazil (Poppino & Schneider, 2019).

Through these efforts, Brazil became relevant to the Portuguese. The Portuguese turned some areas, like Pernambuco, into sugar-producing powerhouses. At the time, sugar was (and still is) a very lucrative commodity. To this day, Brazil still remains a significant sugar producer globally (Shahbandeh, 2021). In the mid-18th Century, gold was discovered. A gold rush ensued, but with a fast depletion of resources, the gold rush ended abruptly. Brazil would depend more on its agricultural economy for success producing coffee, sugar, cotton, and tobacco.

These developments led to an influx of enslaved Africans to Brazil. The population of enslaved people in the new government was double that of Europeans. Sugar production is a very labor-intensive process that the Portuguese needed laborers to perform in their mills and the land. Their labor shortage and lack of capital also made buying enslaved people the solution with the most economic sense. Africans ended up in Brazil precisely because of this reason.

At the turn of the 17th Century, Brazil developed further. The Portuguese instilled government systems in Brazil, similar to those in Portugal. Brazil was becoming an attractive place for people to migrate to. One of the first groups to get there were the Jesuits, an order of the Roman Catholic Church, who made it their priority, among other things, to bring natives and other populations into Christianity. As such, Catholicism found roots in Brazil.

The Jesuits would come to have a significant influence on the natives, to such an extent that the colonists, who needed natives to supplement other sources of labor, resented them and got into conflict with them. Factors that exacerbated the situation were epidemics. Making fewer natives able to work and reducing their population—Europeans and natives alike were inflicted by diseases that had no immunity (Poppino & Schneider, 2019).

Portugal's control of Brazil was not always problem-free. From the get-go, there were attempts by the Dutch and the French to wrestle control of Brazil from their hands. The Dutch and the French would ultimately end up unsuccessful, even after 25-year ownership of Pernambuco. The need to unify and fortify Brazil became ever more significant to the Portuguese and Spain (who briefly united from 1580 t0 1640). Despite the vastness of Brazil, those who lived under the Portuguese, despite differences in race, tradition, or ancestry, believed they shared identity because of the language and inherited colonial norms. This would become the seeds for their national identity.

Many enslaved people who came to Brazil were from West Africa, as far down as Angola. They took their culture and religious beliefs with them when they came to Brazil. Enslaved people were either prisoners of war, captured, handed over to slave traders to pay debts, paid tribute to a chief, or exchanged for food by a community.

The Religious System

Catholicism was introduced to Brazil during the arrival of the Portuguese and the Jesuits. It was made the only official, legal religion. Natives, enslaved people, and everyone else was required to pay tithes to the Catholic Church and abide by its norms. There was no religious freedom. So, conversions of natives and enslaved people from their religion were compulsory.

Enslaved people who arrived in Brazil and wanted to keep their religious beliefs and practices had to do so in private or disguise their faith by fusing elements of Catholicism with

African spiritualism. Later, as other people voluntarily moved to Brazil, religious laws were relaxed. Freedom of religion was allowed, but Catholicism remained the nation's official religion, meaning the church got money from the government and was still heavily involved in politics and governing.

It was only later, in 1891, that the church was separated from the government with the first constitution of the republic. However, the church was still very influential despite the separation. For instance, divorce was outlawed in Brazil up until 1977, mainly because of opposition by the Catholic Church.

More than 64% of the Brazilian population is Catholic, while 22% is Protestant/Pentecostal. Christianity is dominant because of the initial religious intolerance of European colonialism. Today, Brazil is a much more vibrant place since freedom of religion was established in the 19th Century despite apparent Christian domination. Other non-Christian faiths in Brazil include Judaism, Islam, Buddhism, Shinto, Rastafarianism, Candomblé, which is the subject of this book, and Umbanda (Meyer, 2014).

TWO

The Perceptions of Good and Evil

LET'S ACKNOWLEDGE THE BIAS THAT MOST CONVERSATIONS ON conceptions of good and evil suffer from. Usually, the discussion of good and evil tries to explain the origins of evil rather than the origins of good. Goodness is taken as a given, and evil is an aberration to how things should be. So, not a lot is written explaining goodness, while a lot is written to explain evil. I don't know why this bias exists or if it's philosophically justified. Many conversations about good and evil are often about conservation and evil. I am not immune to that bias, so most of this section will be dedicated to explaining African religions' and, by extension, Afro-Brazilian religions' conception of evil. We will contrast that with Christian notions of good and evil to better understand the difference. Remember, some differences may be diminished or removed in some examples of African religion interpretation or literature because of Christian influence.

The divergence in the conception of evil, explicitly explaining it, begins with the starting point of both faiths: namely, their concept of the Supreme Being. You have an intentional God about his creation in the Christian faith and have clear moral expectations and requirements. In the bible, we have God laying out the law many times, but the most famous ones are the Ten Commandments and "do unto others" by Jesus Christ. Both are clear moral statements.

Explaining evil is complicated for this conception of a Supreme Being because it makes people wonder: If God is all-powerful and good. He wants good things. Why doesn't He just get rid of evil? Either God is not omnipotent, which would explain why he can't get rid of evil, or he is not good, which would explain the existence of evil, or he doesn't exist, or he doesn't care about evil. Christians can't accept any of these possibilities because they all contradict the dominant theology: God is good, all-powerful, and all-knowing, he cares, and he exists.

But think about it, if I came to you. I said I was a king of a nation with absolute power to change the law, and I struggled to outlaw something. You might be right in thinking I don't have unlimited power.

The Supreme Being, envisioned by West African religions and its derivatives, does not have moral goals regarding his creation. Evil can exist because of a disinterested God. It wouldn't pose the same problem with a morally specific God. Think about it. If a deist God created the universe, and he had no expectations for life or his creation, he would not care either way if evil exists or not. The deist Supreme Being not caring doesn't mean the gods under him, or we can't care.

In western African theology, the Orixás are concerned with keeping things a certain way or engendering a moral code. There is no reason to think that the Supreme Being, as conceived by Africans, is highly interested in all this work.

Christian theology and African theology also differ in their characterization of evil. The devil and demons are the primary agents of evil in the Christian worldview. They are fundamentally evil—as if evil is in their nature. Africans believe there are evil spirits, but these spirits are understood as being wronged or holding a grudge, which is why they wish to do harm. Nobody thinks they are evil by nature.

To illustrate what I mean, imagine the devil comes to you and offers you a million dollars. He says to you, "I really hate seeing you suffer. I need you to have a happy and prosperous life. I think this money would be beneficial in making that happen." Many people would not take that deal or be highly skeptical over his intentions simply because they think the devil is incapable of doing anything good. But in African theology, an evil spirit can conceivably do something good because it is still capable of change.

Take Exú as an example. He has done many morally questionable things. However, people still believe he is helpful and capable of doing good things. No one thinks Exú is fundamentally evil or fundamentally good. They are just who they are. Deal with the devil tales exists in African culture, but they aren't created to illustrate how corrupt some spirits are. Africans see evil as fundamentally grounded in the transgression of norms set by humans and the gods, not God's will because there is no will. Things just are.

As a result, those in Candomblé don't make sharp distinctions between good and evil. Restoring balance and nurturing the life force Exú is of the most importance. Thus, the moral prescriptions of Candomblé emphasize reciprocity and traditional and ancestral obligation.

THREE

The Five Nations of Candomblé

THE CONCEPT OF CULTURAL HERITAGE HAS EVOLVED significantly over the last few decades. The word used to solely designate prominent remnants of civilizations. In reality, cultural heritage has a broader meaning today. It includes the most beautiful monuments and intangible elements that have long disappeared along with civilizations. They have been preserved and transmitted by societies for centuries, often without being fully recognized as such. This is especially true for Candomblé, a religion of West African origin.

Candomblé is a religion developed in Brazil among enslaved Africans during the 16th century. The word Candomblé, in the Yoruba language, means "house of worship." The basis of Candomblé spirituality is centered on a Supreme Being called Oludumaré, who created everything that exists but does not interfere with daily life. This divine force is found in Orixás - deities and ancestral spirits that can be both male and female. They represent the forces of nature and cannot be fully recognized as good or bad, as they all have both positive and negative features.

The Orixás govern everything on Earth according to the principles of harmony, justice, and truth. It is believed that if respect is not given to them, through worship and devotion called terês, they will bring misfortune and chaos upon their believers. The deities also serve as guidance for human life; for example, Omolu (Yemonja) deals with illnesses such as malaria while Iansã (Iemanjá) deals with storms at sea. Each deity requires a particular shrine within the Candomblé temple called an ialô, where its followers (iyalorixás) offer gifts and pray for their guidance and protection.

The iyalorixás are the spiritual leaders of any Candomblé community. They lead religious services and rituals during ceremonies that last all night long. A noticeable aspect of the Candomblé religion is its use of music in ceremonies, including drumming using various instruments such as agogô, atabaque, and chocalho. The songs often reflect history through narratives about the deities and their lives. Several Candomblé songs are shared with other Afro-Brazilian religions such as samba de roda (Candomblé de Angola), batuque (Umbanda) and aboio (Xangô).

For years, Candomblé was an oral tradition that passed knowledge through storytelling. Over time, practices have become more codified, increasing their resemblance to Santeria in Cuba or voodoo in Haiti because it has many similar traditions and beliefs. However, it also differs from these two religions in many ways. While Santeria and voodoo were influenced by the slave trade, Candomblé is directly linked to African rituals, tradition, and worship.

Enslaved people brought traditional African practices with them to Brazil. They mixed them into an emerging religious system that would later develop into Candomblé. The first enslaved West Africans arrived in Brazil around 1530. Still, it wasn't until 1549 that the first terreiro (Afro-Brazilian house of worship) was founded. By the end of the 17th century, more than thirty terreiros in Salvador, Bahia.

Initially, enslaved people who wanted to practice Candomblé had to sneak away from their plantations and attend ceremonies. Later, terreiros were built in the woods surrounding towns and plantations because other Afro-Brazilians became interested in this religion. By 1800, there were 400 terreiros in Bahia alone.

Candomblé is divided into 5 nations. The term "nations" refers to various groups sharing the same basic principles and beliefs of the Candomblé tradition but still different from each other in many respects. The next chapters will discuss Ketu Candomblé Nation, Ijexá Nation, Jeje Nation, Bantu Nation, and Caboclô Nation.

Ketu Candomblé Nation

The Ketu Nation is the oldest of the nations, coming from the Yoruba nation. They keep their culture strictly separate from other countries while practicing the Ketu cult exclusively. It is one of the largest, most commonly known Candomblé groups. The Ketu Nation was established in Salvador, Brazil. It has many temples throughout Brazil and is very well known overseas. The principles of the group are based on traditional African religion, with an emphasis on secrecy and respect for other nations.

The nation has three distinct branches: Ketu-Ijexa (original), Ketu Axé Opô Afonjá, and Ketu Axé Ipanapin. All three groups believe in one God called Nana Buluku, the creator of everything that exists. In West Africa, there was a belief that each chief or king had a personal god who successfully helped rule their people. The high priest of this god was also considered to have special abilities from his God. This belief spread with the enslaved people when they were taken from Africa to Brazil via the Atlantic Ocean slave trade during the 17th and 18th centuries.

During this time, the enslavers did not want their slaves practicing any form of religion because it would make them resistant to enslavement. To keep their traditional ways alive, some groups held separate secret ceremonies apart from other Candomblé groups, while others had more centralized traditions. The Ketu Nation was one of these groups that separated themselves for fear of persecution during slavery times.

Although each nation has different beliefs and traditions, the Ketu Nation is known for one thing in particular: its openness to other cultures and religions. They are the only nation that practices polygamy and allows members of any race or religion to join them as long as they accept certain aspects of African spirituality. They also seem to be more open about their rituals than other nations. Some outsiders, such as Americans, have been able to see what goes on inside a ritual room while it's happening rather than just seeing statues or pictures afterward. This openness gives them an edge when recruiting new members who feel like they don't belong anywhere else. This group seems like a place where anyone can fit in and will not be judged for their beliefs or backgrounds.

Although not all members agree on every aspect of the religion, most people hold some beliefs about this group. The nation is led by a high priest who is referred to as Pã atã – father of fire. This title comes from the king of Ketu, who was consulted by Olófin about rituals and beliefs during slavery times. He was given special powers to lead his people. Still, he had to stay hidden from those searching for enslaved people practicing religion or those purposely trying to destroy Ketu Candomblé. This title has been passed down through the years and never officially given to anyone, making it difficult for outside investigators to confirm who currently holds this title.

Many other nations practice Candomblé, but the Ketu Nation is unique because they don't have a central religious text or book of rituals like most others do. This lack of a "bible" gives different groups freedom to make up their own traditions and expand on what already exists instead of going by something officially written down somewhere else. They also believe strongly in ancestor worship. Passed down through oral tradition and stories shared within each group, making it seem more authentic than if there was just one set way of doing things. Especially since those who have died cannot write about their experiences during life. Ketu Candomblé continues to grow and evolve each day with no sign of slowing down anytime soon. Revealing its importance to the people who practice it and their desire to keep carrying on ancient traditions.

Ijexá Candomblé Nation

The Ijexa Nation was founded by three people who escaped Nigeria together in 1835, after the defeat of Dahomey to Porto-Novo. Ijexá is composed of ije, which means "land," and exa, meaning "pour." The Ijexá is also called the Shango cult group. Yoruba mythology is named after one of their principal deities, Xangô or Changó, the God of Lightning and Fire. He was brought to Brazil by enslaved people from Nigeria.

The Ijexa people believe in a supreme deity, called Oludumaré or Olorun. They consider themselves the children of Oranmiyan (also known as Oriyomi), Xangô's half-brother. The Ijexá are also polytheists who worship many deities with different functions in their lives. They are sometimes distinguished by the colors of their clothes or Adinkra symbols they use to decorate their bodies. However, it is more common for them to differentiate themselves according to the Orixás they worship.

The Ijexá believe in reincarnation, and their practices include aspects comparable to those of animism, such as divination with cowrie shells. The Ijexa people wear white or black robes with red, yellow, or green borders during ceremonies related to Shango. They often participate in Candomblé festivals, especially the festivals of Iansã and Ogun, who is considered the God responsible for creating weapons and war.

The Ijexá people believe that those who do not wear adornments honoring Shango will never find true love. The Portuguese once tried to force them to abandon their religious beliefs as Catholics, but they were unsuccessful after numerous battles. Because of this resistance, they became known as "warriors.

They are organized into small groups led by babalawôs. Only men can be initiated in the group, representing one godhead. Still, they cannot practice if they do not respect women and nature, which they find sacred. Women are represented by Ogans, who are occasionally initiated as priestesses. They can also lead a group, but they must be accompanied by a man who heads the ritualistic ceremonies and songs.

They perform rituals through dance, songs, and percussion instruments like drums called "ogãs," congas, and bells to communicate with the gods. Their musical tradition is vibrant. It includes different types of rhythms that can be divided into three categories. Toques de Santo (drums used in rituals), toques de Congo (ritual songs), e toques de Ijexá (traditional songs of the Ijexá nation).

It is also interesting to know that they respect people with disabilities, considered special messengers between humans and deities. The Ijexá Nation is found throughout Brazil but mainly in Bahia state. They have over 60 branches called tijolos (bricks) or terreiros (temples).

Jejé Candomblé Nation

The Indigenous West African people called Yorubas came to Brazil in the 16th century. These enslaved people were called "Nago," which comes from their language word "to go." Thanks to this linguistic similarity, they integrated with other peoples in Brazil, mainly Tupinambas and Angola-Congos, who were already here. After centuries of historical events - such as slave rebellions or immigration by other Africans - these people started creating new cultural elements that would be part of their identity.

The Jejé Nation has its own culture, history, and language. It's rich enough to compete with others in Brazil and other countries, including arts (dance, theater, music), cuisine (African food includes dishes like Moqueca, Acarajé or Okra Creole), literature (like traditional songs or religious writings), and religion (Candomblé). This discovery of their roots gave them a strong sense of affirmation to face life ahead, building on earlier foundations. For this reason, they became known as "Brazilians with African roots."

Jejé Candomblé Nation has the following founding principles: Affirmation − Promoting and disseminating culture and tradition; Culture − Preservation and development; Education − Instilling self-knowledge and traditional values to build a healthy personality; Communication - To ensure visibility; Learning - To know oneself through research; Struggle for Justice - To denounce any type of discrimination.

This religion stands out because it does not discriminate against color, age, or social status (for the poorest people).

However, its followers must respect each sect, as each has its distinctive features. The objective is to work with unity, respecting each other and the right of everyone to be different.

This religion also has a spiritual service called Lavagem. People are washed with scented water, sandalwood powder, and lemongrass oil. This is done by women who work as "Mães de Santo" (Mothers or Heads of Saint) - they not only serve food and drinks at ceremonies but care for the children and adolescents there.

In Jejé Nation, there are no rigid rules on how a ceremony should go. Everything depends on your Orixás, which is why they need to communicate with each practitioner through a symbiotic relationship called "Ponto." This is carried out with the assistance of a spiritual leader who will read for you at that time.

This symbiosis brings about different types of work called "Arruadas," where people are possessed by their Orixás. This is done through songs and dances - some are slow, others are fast. During this, your body will start to move differently depending on how strong the energy feels. This symbiosis can also bring about knowledge from beyond or help with divination techniques during ceremonies.

Bantu Candomblé Nation

The Bantu Candomblé Nation is a secretive religion that has been practiced by the Olmec, Yoruba, Fon/Ewe, Xinca, and Igbo people for thousands of years. Bantu Candomblé worshippers have been persecuted by Christian missionaries and governments in Africa, South America, and North America. Since many nations have criminalized native religions, they are forced to continue their faith in secret or leave for Brazil or another country where it is legal.

The exact number of Bantu Candomblé followers is unknown, but maybe between 100,000 and 200,000. Followers are concentrated primarily in Brazil and exist in Nigeria, Portugal, the United States of America, Suriname, French Guiana, and the Netherlands.

Worshippers believe in a Supreme Being known as Nana Buluku. She is prayed to and worshiped through her multitude of avatars, including the sun, moon, stars, and other natural phenomena. The primary avatar of Nana Buluku is Yemonja, who created humans from clay on a potter's wheel like the Abrahamic God does in the Book of Genesis. Like some ancient Mediterranean peoples, she was once married. Still, she chose to be celibate like some Hindu gods are believed to be. It is common for Bantu Candomblé worshippers (known as Ifá) to honor multiple religions at once. Bantu mythology states that all major religions, including Christianity and Islam, were brought by Ifá and contain a kernel of truth.

Yorubas believe that all souls must travel to Òrun (the spiritual realm) after death, judged by an old god known as Orunmila. Bantu myth states Orunmila existed before Yemonja and gave her the power to create life on Earth and the ability to revive those who had passed away by using calabash. It resembles gourds such as pumpkin or squash filled with enchanted water.

In addition to Yemonja, Orishas are not gods but spiritual beings who help humans on Earth. Some of the most prominent Orishas include Obatala, who is worshipped as a god and goddess by those seeking beauty, creativity, and art. Ifá priests have been sent to Earth by Yemonja and Orunmila during the early days (after creation). These became known as Babalawôs (priests- doctors). While occupying human bodies, they help humans understand their destiny through divination, meditation, and prayer.

Bantus have numerous festivals that honor different deities each month. These include Ogun's festival, which occurs during the dry season when less food is available for humans and animals alike. During this time, hunters take part in an annual ritual where they pray for safety before traveling into the forest to find a game; failure to make this journey could result in starvation. The first festival is dedicated to Yemonja and before other celebrations begins. Because she is responsible for bringing forth various food products, humans can stockpile enough resources to survive the additional twelve months of the year.

Other ceremonies are held to protect crops, villages, families, and even individual homes. Each deity has its own specific role that it must play during these rituals. They are said to influence different aspects of life on Earth. If someone worships one god, his power may be diminished by not honoring all deities equally. Bantus have also created a unique system where male priests called Babalawôs can become initiated as female priestesses called Iyalorishas. The latter can "marry" the god of their choice.

Caboclô Candomblé Nation

During colonial times, the Caboclôs were brought to Brazil as enslaved people by Portuguese settlers. The first waves arrived in 1549, followed by others who came up till 1825 when slavery was finally abolished throughout Brazil.' caboclô' means 'one with an indigenous soul.'

The nation Caboclô was born out of Jejé but also significantly diverged from Mestre Irineu's beliefs because of his intense devotion towards Catholicism. This nation worships spirits known as "Pretos Velhos," African deities who do not follow Catholic practices and were said to be enslaved Black Brazilians themselves.

During their religious ceremonies, followers wear white costumes with colorful headdresses to mimic the dress of these African deities. This nation is essential because it also represents the importance of geographical location in determining how religious groups function and develop over time. For example, Caboclô developed from Jejé primarily due to its geographic location- meaning that there were more descendants from Africa living in Rio de Janeiro than in Bahia, where Mestre Irineu created his original form of Candomblé.

The Caboclô Candomblé Nation maintains African practices such as polygamy (which many ancient African tribes), animal sacrifice for initiation ceremonies and burials, and wearing white clothing during special occasions. This nation establishes an idea of what it means to be black abroad. They are concerned about discrimination against women, colorism (preference given to lighter skin tones) within their own community, and preserving traditional practices. This group's existence can also symbolize hope for building bridges between communities; it is an example of how different people can come together for a common purpose.

The traditional African religions that the members practice are Vodou, Candomblé, and Umbanda that developed in Brazil (note: these three traditions are all practiced in Haiti). These religions use the gods associated with Yorubaland. This place was located near Nigeria, where many West Africans were referred to as caboclôs or 'brown ones' because they had not lost their connection with nature.

The traditions utilize trance experiences to heal illness. There are several similarities between these practices and European pagan traditions or Western occult tradition, including belief in nature as a force, ritual use of drums and dance, and emphasis on the individual.

The five nations that make up Candomblé are all very different. Still, they intertwine to create a complex system of worship and belief. The Ketu nation has been at the forefront of bringing about change within the Candomblé community and changing how many people outside of Brazil perceive this religion. Ijexá is much more conservative in its practices and involvement with politics than Caboclô or Jejé. Bantu focus much more on the spiritual aspects of the faith rather than political involvement. Each nation has both traditional and modern elements. Still, certain factors differ from nation to nation, depending on those factions' preferences.

The central belief of Candomblé is that there are many spirits represented by the Orishas, who form a pantheon of divinities. These serve in much the same manner as Christians' "God" and include human beings and animals, plants, and stones, all of which have an essence and life force.

FOUR

The Supreme Being

CANDOMBLÉ COSMOLOGY IS SIMILAR TO THAT OF WEST African religions. To better understand the topics we will discuss and avoid confusion, I will contrast Candomblé's ideas with popular Christian ideas.

Olorun

Olorun, sometimes called Oludumaré, is the Supreme Being of the Yoruba people and, by extension, the God of Candomblé. Olorun serves as an example of Candomblé's conception of a Supreme Being or god. Later, we will discuss differences in Candomblé nations as they relate to the Supreme Being. Olorun means "one who lives in the sky." He is considered a sky god, but he is also credited with creating the universe and omnipotent.

In simple terms, Olorun is as big as the Christian God. Still, there is an essential difference between him and Christian conceptions of God in the level of involvement in everyday life and intentionality. The significant similarity between the

Christian conception of God and Olorun is in their statues as "necessary beings" (more on this soon).

Olorun is more of a deist god. In other words, he is not involved in the day-to-day happenings of the universe. The story of how Olorun created the universe paints him as someone distant. He gives a lesser god, Obatala, resources to build the world and delivers instructions. For instance, when making humans, he gives the god clay to shape into human form, which they do. Then, Olorun completes the process by breathing life into the clay. Olorun is the source of the life force and the universe, but he doesn't act in the universe. He leaves responsibility for all things in the universe to the lower gods he created. The Christian conception of God is more involved than this. In it, God has goals and aspirations for humans and acts in the world through angels or directly to make things happen. The Christian God, like in most monotheist religions, is interventionist.

This brings us to the second difference. It's evident in the Christian conception of God that God has some overarching purpose. In other words, God is intentional with anything he does. Olorun is not portrayed as having an overriding agenda. The only thing that could be said about him with certainty is that he wants to maintain balance and orderliness in the universe. Still, he does not do so himself—all the lesser gods are in charge of that.

One does not pray directly to Olorun; He is too distant and uninvolved to do anything. There are no rituals, ceremonies, or shrines built in his name. But humans, if they want, can have prayers sent to him. Now, it's at this point that some people find it depressing, but it isn't. All the gods that Olorun has spread over the universe are enough for any sort of spiritual connection that people may need or want. People have positive feelings towards Olorun because he is a good God who gave them everything in existence, including life itself. An essential similarity with the Christian God is that the universe's presence depends on them—they are necessary beings.

Necessary being is a concept in the philosophy of religion that posits that there must exist a being that the entire universe depends on. Whether they are valid or not, the rationale behind this concept is not the focus of this book. The first reason is that all things that exist cannot be dependent—a reason for existing—on other things for their existence. For instance, if I asked you where sand comes from, you might say from stones. If I asked where stones come from, you might say geological activities within the Earth and space. Whatever answer you give, I can keep asking about what the next thing comes from. The point is: The whole collection of things can't all come from, or depend on, other things to be; otherwise, we will have an infinite regression that can't be a physical reality. So, along that chain of causation, there has to be a thing that depends on itself for its existence, and everything else depends on it to exist. It is the starting point of all that exists—that thing is a necessary being because, without it, nothing would be.

Another way religious philosophers come to the same conclusion is by asking themselves: why does something exist rather than nothing? In this instance, nothingness means absolute nothing—the absence of matter, space, time, and energy. The answer becomes: There is something. After all, there can be nothing because there exists a being whose existence is necessary. In other words, a being whose non-existence is impossible. I am simplifying here, but that is essentially the answer. Olorun and the Christian God have self-existence—necessary being-ness—in common.

The Yoruba Candomblé nations of Ketu and Ijexá nations refer to their Supreme Being as Olorun (obviously). The Supreme Being of Jejé Candomblé, having found their religion from the enslaved people of the Fon and Ewe, is Nana-Baluku. Her story is different from Olorun's, but she is still deist and self-existent, just like Olorun. Although she created the universe, she left the creation of everything else to two gods. She gave birth to Mawu and Lisa. Sometimes, they are portrayed as the same god with two different sides. All the other gods are thought to have descended from Mawu and Lisa, making them the sovereigns.

The Bantu Candomblé nation gets its pantheon and cosmology from the Kongo religion. Bantu people are ethnic groups in Africa who speak Bantu languages. They migrated from Central Africa to southeast Africa and southern Africa. More than 22 countries in Africa are predominantly composed of Bantu-speaking peoples, including 97% of Congo and 97% of Angola.

My point is that Bantu Candomblé is composed of essentially the same people, despite hundreds of Bantu-speaking tribes. So, adopting predominantly Congo pantheon and beliefs in the Bantu Candomblé, even if you were Mbundu (Angolan), was not a stretch. You can go as deep as South Africa to ask the people there to recognize the concepts and some of the pantheon presented in Kongo Religion. I bet you they will say they do. Many beliefs and practices are strikingly similar despite thousands of years of separation and hundreds of years of colonial rule. That alone is a fantastic achievement. Of course, there are many differences, but the core beliefs remain unusually the same. For instance, the Basotho people of Lesotho, deep in Southern Africa, believe in spirits, a Supreme Being, diviners, healers, witches, and ancestors. Which are similar (not equivalent) to those in the Kongo religion.

Nzambi Kalunga, sometimes called Nzambi Mpungu, is the Supreme Being of the Kongo religion. He is credited with creating the universe and is omnipotent. He is also a deist. In his origin story, he became bored of his own creation and left, but he is still the life source of the universe as we know it. For instance, he causes rain to fall, helps in the birth of children, makes seeds grow into food that people can eat, and so on. In other words, he is the working hand behind all of nature, keeping things working like clockwork. His deist nature comes from his disinterest in human affairs. He is impartial, just like the laws of physics. People in the Congo religion do not pray to him or seek his favor because he is not the kind of god to accept worship (Asante & Mazama, 2008).

Nzambici is another god sent to Earth by Nzambi Mpungu. She later married Nzambi Mpungu. She is mother to all animals and gave humanity laws, arts, games, and music. She plays a more active role in the affairs here at home. Similarly, she carried on to Bantu Candomblé with Nzambi Mpungu being the Supreme Being and Nzambici acting as the god here on Earth (Asante & Mazama, 2008).

Given Candomblé's conceptions of God, it is simple to see why Candomblé, unlike Christianity, is not a salvation-based religion where human beings need saving from eternal damnation. The idea of original sin and needing to repent were probably very strange to those who practiced African religions. First, they were confronted with an almighty God. Similar in some ways to their ideas of a Supreme Being who cared a great deal about human affairs in a way that was new to them. Secondly, the whole needed to be saved from eternal damnation, which disagreed with their cosmology or an understanding of how the life cycle works. Many African people today still hold on to African ideas about life, death, rituals, and traditions even if they are professed Christians. For instance, they are still more likely to do rituals to please ancestors or other patron spirits during the death of a loved one or the birth of a child.

To summarize, all Candomblé versions have an idea of a deist omnipotent supreme being. Below them are lesser gods, deities who regularly interact with the universe. There is usually a more meaningful and influential god in that pantheon, who is sovereign; it is this good that most followers of Candomblé try to appeal to. The Supreme Being is never petitioned for intervention and yet also highly respected since they are the originator of all existence.

FIVE

The Deified Ancestors

ORIXÁS ARE THE LESSER GODS, CALLED DEITIES, CREATED BY the Supreme Being. There are many Orixás out there, and each has its own role. We will look at three aspects of Orixás: Who they are, what their function is, and why people worship them. Although there are hundreds of Orixás out there, a few of them are the most revered and appear in almost all significant celebrations or rituals.

Different Candomblés refer to Orixás by other names on linguistic and ethnic grounds, but they refer to the same entities. Different nations or temples may worship a different set of Orixás or all of them. As we have said, the word Orixás, referring to deities, is recognized across all Candomblés to refer to gods. So, we will use the Yoruba pantheon monikers as our entry point.

The general role of Orixás is to act as intermediaries between people and the Supreme Being. Since everything in existence is imbued with a sacred energy/life force from the Supreme Being, these deities connect to that well of power and connection. The sacred energy/life force from the Supreme Being is referred to as ax. There are sixteen significant Orixás, but we will focus on these 10 because they are ubiquitous: Exú, Oxalá, Xangô, Oxóssi, Ogum, Omolu, Iemanjá, Oxunmare, Oxum, and Iansã.

In Candomblé, people are believed to be born with a specific connection to a single Orixás or many. These Orixás become their guardians, and their relationship with them must be maintained through prayers and occasional sacrifices. Orixás are not too demanding unless people are called to serve them. Orixás also have sacred days. People with a natural affinity to an Orixás or a devotee are sometimes referred to as children of that deity, which sometimes comes with certain expectations. Natural affinity to an Orixás is often spotted by a person's personality type and behavior in a manner akin to astrological signs.

Exú

Exú is understood to be a messenger and guardian of crossroads. He is often considered an outside Orixás because most of what he does is look after temples, houses, cities, and crossroads. His primary role is that of communication. Exú opens communication between humans and the gods. Sometimes, he functions as a messenger between the gods too.

Exú is a gatekeeper. During ceremonies, nothing can be done without offering sacrifices to him. Once a connection is established, other Orixás may be invited. Exú is one of the most exciting Orixás personalities because he embodies many human qualities. In African tradition, stories about his cunningness, indecency, funniness, and trickery abound. He is considered intelligent, lively, and never willing to turn down a party. He is also lecherous and gluttonous. Exú is neither a good nor evil god; he is just who he is. He is often represented by red and black colors.

In Vodun, Exú is recognized as Legba or Papa Legba. His presentation always shows him with a large, erect penis to symbolize his lust and a tendency to overindulge. Sacrifices to Legba or other versions of him are never considered excessive. Exú's sexual side is less emphasized in Candomblé because of Catholic influence. However, the older version of this statue still represents him with a large, erect penis.

Children of Exú are gregarious, unique, and don't follow societal norms. They are often playful, witty, and not afraid to get into trouble for some fun. Exú's sacred day is Monday. His elements are fire or earth, and his symbol is an ogó, a penis-shaped stick that is sometimes adorned with balls. Exú will accept animal sacrifices like goats and roosters, but sometimes cavies and snails. Exú's special greeting is Laroiê, Exu.

Oxalá

Oxalá is the oldest and the most respected of all the Orixás. We mentioned them in our section on Olorun with another name: Obatala. Olorun tasks him with creating the Earth, humans, and everything in it, and then Olorun breathes life into humans. All the other gods are children of Oxalá, so he is sometimes referred to as the father of Orixás. Oxalá's mythology is illustrious because of the central role he plays in setting up the Yoruba pantheon.

Oxalá is represented by the color white to symbolize purity and creativity. Creativity in the creation sense, not the artful senses, gives the nod to his name, which means "white ox." The color blue, mixed with white, represents Oxalá. Oxalá is sometimes portrayed in two ways: the young and old versions. The young version of Oxalá is called Oxagulã, and his symbol is a sword, white pestle, and shield. In earthly form, he is simply called Oxalufã, and his symbol is a metal staff.

Because of mythological reasons, alcohol, salt, palm oil, and coal are restricted to his children. For instance, Oxalá oil should have palm oil or salt. In various stories, there is some conflict between Exú and Oxalá because of Exú's trickery when Oxalá was tasked with creating the world. Any symbols that represent Exú, like red and black clothes, should not be worn by Oxalá devotees. Oxalá's sacred days are on Friday and Sunday. On these days, devotees should avoid eating food with salt in them—others have chosen not to eat meat, but white food, like fish, can be eaten.

The children of Oxalá are characterized by their aversion to conflict and disorder. They like quiet, order, and peace and enjoy getting along well with others. Psychologists would call agreeable and conscientious because they are organized and work well with others.

Xangô

Xangô is the Orixá of lightning, thunder, and fire, representing wrath and power. For that reason, he is thought to symbolize passion and temper. All this explosiveness is connected to ideas of justice. Many understand that Xangô is a God who enforces and establishes justice, consistent with Candomblé's emphasis on balance. Xangô's role is to establish justice which requires ire. Xangô punishes anyone who behaves unfairly, immorally or takes advantage of others.

If you feel wronged, he is the god you would petition for intervention. Xangô is considered brave and righteous because of his power and willingness to right wrongs. He has powers of wizardry while being a great combatant, and he is a tyrant king of the legendary city of Oyo. Some may say that Xangô is the most feared of the gods.

Xangô is represented by red, white, and brown. His sacred day is Wednesday, and the elements ascribed to him are fire, storms, sun, thunder, earthquakes, lightning, volcanoes, deserts, and rock formations. His domains are justice, law, governance, and state. He accepts tortoise, amala, lamb, and goat as offerings.

The children of Xanga are often characterized by their arrogance. They don't like being disrespected, are very passionate, and want to have the last word. They are not comfortable with being alone. They may seem bold and selfish, but they usually have a strong sense of justice, and they will protect and stand up for the vulnerable. They won't take nonsense from anyone.

Oxóssi

Oxóssi is the god of hunting, animals, forests, and sustenance. He is also considered to be a patron of the arts. Oxóssi is a hunter himself, often praised for being a great hunter and always eating game (a reference to how good a hunter is). Believers see him as a provider of all food. He is considered the god of agriculture too.

He protects the hunter (providers and workers) and the hunt (the work itself). For this reason, he is also considered the god of wealth. So, anyone who works and creates wealth is under the protection of Oxóssi. Because he is a patron of the arts, he is present in art creation. People often consult Oxóssi when faced with work-related problems, financial issues, a lack of creativity, and unemployment.

Hunting was one of the significant ways that communities got food in Africa and gathered. A good hunt was always appreciated because it helped balanced diets. The meat was beneficial for other things like clothes and blankets. Because Oxóssi is also a forest god, he knows all the herbs that may treat or cure ailments.

Oxóssi is represented by green or light blue. Thursday is his sacred day. His symbols are closely tied to a hunting excursion like bows, arrows, knives, and spears. In his worship, followers of Oxóssi incorporate these items.

The children of Oxóssi are believed to be calm and good at regulating their emotions. When you think about how hard it can be to hunt and the kind of mental fortitude and patience needed to be successful, this makes a lot of sense. So, it is not unusual for his children to be cautious, selective, attentive, and loyal. The loyalty must stem from the teamwork and camaraderie required to be a hunter of a tribe.

Ogum

Ogum is the god of iron, metallurgy, technology, and war. When people hear words like these strewn together, they don't feel very positive about that god. Nonetheless, he plays a critical role: in protecting communities and the advancement of civilization. He watches a community of people by giving them the technology and weapons to defend themselves from whoever wishes to destroy them. Advancing civilization includes positive things like new inventions that make life long and worthwhile. Its color is green.

Ogum is believed to be fearless and aggressive; he is persistent and fights against anyone or anything that dares challenge him. He symbolizes strength, perseverance, and triumph in great difficulty. People seek his guidance when they are faced with great danger. Warriors going to war would ask for his favor, so would people who live in dangerous neighborhoods in need of extra protection.

Children of Ogum are often quick to engage in conflict without needing an explanation. With short tempers, they don't let go of things quickly. They have a strong fighting spirit and will often try things even when the odds are against them. They are not afraid of struggle and are often praised for being resilient in adversity. They make good, inspiring leaders.

Iemanjá

Iemanjá is perhaps the most popular of the Orixás celebrated in many regions. She is considered the mother of almost all Orixás. She is the goddess of the seas and maternity, a protector of children, the elderly, and a patron of fishermen. She also controls destiny. She goes by many epithets like the Yoruba's "mother whose children are fish." Her colors are clear blue, silver, and green. She is strongly associated with fluid bodies of water like rivers.

Her element is water. She does not have a sacred day, but she is prayed to often. She is annually celebrated in huge festivals across Brazil on the 2nd of February and on New Years' Eve in Rio de Janeiro. People of different faiths often gather to celebrate with devotees.

Her domain is over the seas, womanhood, fertility, and family. She is often portrayed wearing blue, white, or both—sometimes with fish or as a mermaid. Offerings made to her vary, but they all represent femininity: flowers, jewelry, lipstick, mirrors, coconut puddings, and sweet rice. These offerings are made to the sea, and if the goddess rejects them, they are washed back up. You will receive her blessing if she accepts your offering (Grimond, 2017).

The children of Iemanjá love luxury and extravagance, but they are wise and emotionally intelligent. They are confrontational when necessary, always willing to help others. Family-

33

oriented people take care of those who rely on them and have excellent maternal instincts.

Omolu

Omolu is the Orixá of death, smallpox, and other infectious diseases. He is known to cause illness. In fact, he is also the god of fighting against disease. Although Omolu is responsible for healing the sick, he is also responsible for death. His colors are black, white, and red.

Omolu has a dualistic nature because he can also cause disease. However, he wants people to be healthy and rid of infection because of his own suffering. According to myth, Omolu was born sickly, and his mother abandoned him to die by the sea. Iemanjá found him, deformed and eaten by crabs, and raised him, teaching him how to cure disease. He knows what pain is and is motivated to fight disease and suffering. On top of all that, he is the only one who can rid the world of bad things because he is a master of death. His mastery over death can be understood in two ways: he can cause anything to die (or not to die), and he brings death on those suffering too much from illness because he does not want them to suffer. For that reason, he is the most feared god and much needed. His life story symbolizes great endurance, despite great suffering. His symbol is a wooden spear, and its elements are earth and fire. His sacred day is Monday.

He is often depicted wearing a straw outfit that covers his body. The only parts of his body that can be seen are his feet and arms. He shines so brightly that any mortal who sets eyes on him will die. His clothing is there to hide his brightness and scars. The brightness connection with a god capable of bringing so much suffering may seem strange to those of other faiths. Still, it is a sign that he is not malevolent and has a great heart.

The children of Omolu are neurotic and prone to great bouts of sadness. They can be pretty harmful. They often complain about the state of their health, whether mental or physical, but they soldier on. Children of Omolu are not afraid of suffering because they are very familiar with it. They can be pretty hopeless, believing that they will never get any better at times. However, they are sensitive to the needs and pain of others and very affectionate and caring. They are empathetic friends who will go the extra mile for you for those reasons. Because Omolu's children often have to work against their limitations to get things done, they are not afraid of hard work.

Oxunmare

Oxunmare is the keeper of the rainbow. He lives in the sky and travels down to earth using a rainbow. He is symbolized by the rainbow snake, associated with fortune, wealth, and prosperity. Agility and mobility, which are qualities of a snake, are prevalent aspects of the god. He is well known for his wisdom and mental acuity. He is represented by the colors of the rainbow. Oxunmare also represents renewal and regeneration. He can be approached for fortune, money, and growth problems.

His symbols are a double-headed spread or iron serpent. The double-headed serpent represents the coming together of direct opposites, usually the male and female energies. He does not have a sacred day of the week, but he is celebrated on the 24th of August.

The children of Oxunmare are open-minded or androgynous, having qualities of all genders. They are known for their openness and bisexuality. They embrace change in all domains and actively seek it. They are comfortable with uncertainty and differences. Often driven people who are adaptable are always willing to do whatever is necessary to get what they want.

Oxum

Oxum is the goddess of sensuality, fertility, beauty, wealth, and love. She is a youthful goddess, often associated with fresh waters of rivers and streams. Her colors are gold and yellow. Many come to her with relationship problems. Lovers can expect to find comfort and reassurance from her. She is often depicted as an attractive young woman with smooth features. She is the wife of Xangô.

The children of Oxum are agreeable. They respect other people's views, making them excellent at reconciling differences or forming relationships with people different from them. They make great mediators and diplomats. They are kind, sweet, and honest. People feel comfortable and safe in their presence, feeling like they can open up about anything. They are good parents because of these qualities, giving their kids the space they need to grow. They are attracted to peace, calm, and tranquility. They are loyal lovers skilled at developing and advancing the relationship more profoundly and intimately.

Iansã

Iansã is a warrior goddess, also the wife of Xangô. She is the goddess of the winds and is present when winds and water collide in storms and similar events. She is strong and independent. Devotees today think she represents female strength and independence, breaking gender stereotypes. Iansã is as fearless as Xangô. There is also an openness to her which makes her adaptable.

She represents typhoons, the need for change, lighting, and hurricanes.

Her sacred day is Wednesday, and her color is red. In paintings and drawings, she is often portrayed in a storm or wind, wearing a red dress with a sword in her right hand and an ox horn in the other.

The children of Iansã are extroverted and open to new experiences. They love to travel, are very outdoorsy, and can be domineering. They don't like to be undermined and assert themselves if they feel threatened. They are warriors at heart, never backing down from a fight but are not afraid of falling in love (they do this multiple times). They have strong passions and can sometimes struggle with impulsivity. They can also be blunt and aggressive. They can be jealous and possessive and, at the same time, not want intimate relationships.

SIX

Customary Practices in Candomblé

IT IS WORTH BRIEFLY LOOKING AT THE MOST COMMON practices in Candomblé. We have already alluded to some of them in the previous chapter.

Candomblé is often characterized as an initiatory religion. To become priests and other religious practitioners, people must go through an initiation process. The duration of the process and what it entails is unique to the nature of the calling and the authority overseeing it. People who must go through this process are called by the Orixás or ancestors. Signs of a calling can be mental, social, or physical ill-being, which the person seeks to consult about. When they do, an initiate, who is already a practitioner, will take action for that calling to be answered.

That brings us to a common feature in Candomblé: spiritual consultation. When believers, usually ordinary men, and women, are facing a problem—the problem may be financial, mental, physical, interpersonal, or otherwise—they seek out a priest or priestess for intervention in much the same way that a person would go see a doctor if they are sick. The priest and priestess are chosen because of their reputation in the community (Encyclopedia.com, 2018).

When meeting the priest or priestess, a private divination session called a consulta begins where the priest/priestess consults the Orixás by reading cowrie shells called Jogo de búzios. In some African traditions, it is bones instead of cowrie shells, typically from sacrifices, which are shaken and then thrown to the ground to be read and interpreted. The priest/priestess uses the session to diagnose the problem and then offers a solution. For instance, the person seeking assistance might be told that they have an ancestor who is displeased. They may need to perform a sacrifice or ritual to please that ancestor, which will improve. Or, just like we have established, they may be told they need to be initiated into the priesthood for their problems to be resolved. Initiation into priesthood generally means leaving their everyday life behind and dedicating their lives to the service of the Orixás and ancestors. The offering of herbs and instructions on using them are also common interventions alongside sacrifices. In some instances, the followers may ask for such an intervention (Encyclopedia.com, 2018).

Candomblé does not have sacred texts, and almost all knowledge is conveyed through oral traditions.

Temples and Priesthood

Candomblé ceremonies are performed in places called terreiros. Inside terreiros are rooms, some of them off-limits to the uninitiated. These rooms have altars dedicated to Orixás. There is a space for ceremonies, secluding initiates, and accommodation for priests and priestesses. Houses of worship vary by size and wealth. Smaller houses are often priests' homes, and bigger ones are often older and more established. The pole in the middle of the temple is considered a link to the other world. The barracaõ, translated to "big shed," is used for public rituals and divination. Shrines to deities are located on the perimeter of the barracaõ. Smaller temples can use the yard outside as a barracaõ. The barracaõ is often used for big annual celebrations (Encyclopedia.com, 2018).

Duties in the temple are fundamentally different for male and female devotees. Males are often in charge of sacrifices and shaving in rituals and ceremonies. Females are often tasked with more domestic chores. However, females are often leader terreiros; Candomblé is a female-dominated religion. The male priests often do not fit traditional gender norms or are homosexual.

Each temple hosts annual celebrations for the entire patron Orixás, and public members join together in celebration. In these celebrations, initiation members are distinguished by their ritual dresses and jewelry. They perform ritual dancing, pray, and provide offerings to the gods. The Orixás descend upon initiates to either share their consciousness with them or cause the initiates to lose their consciousness temporarily as the Orixás take over. When the Orixás descend, initiates are taken to the back rooms adorned with symbols and colors of the Orixás possessing them.

All terreiros are independent of each other; there is no overarching authority. The head priest or priestess is in charge, not being questioned. Those with more experience are higher in the hierarchy. Younger initiates learn by watching, instruction, and imitation; they aren't permitted to be inquisitive.

Priesthood and Initiation

Candomblé has different types of priesthood. As such, it influences who and how each is initiated. Below you'll find an overview of the different kinds of priesthood.

The head priest or priestess of a terreiros is called mãe or pai de santo; mai de santo is female and pai de santo is male. These are Orixá priests and priestesses. The name translates to mother or father of saints. They are the paternal figures of the house, and those under them are considered their children. The children are called filhoes (sons) or filhas (daughters) de Santo, which translates to "sons or daughters of saints." Each Candomblé nation names these positions by ritual language and tradition. In Jejé Candomblé, the head priest and priestess are called doté and done. In Bantu-based Candomblé, they are called tatankisi and nenguankisi.

Initiation to Candomblé priesthood is bound to differ from other religions because of the sheer number of nations and head priests or priesthoods in charge. However, there are specific patterns that are consistent throughout Candomblé nations. Prospective initiates initially face some problems, as we have established. It is determined by divination that they should be initiated. Once that is established, they are taken to a room to cool off. This may last a week or days. It depends. They are given symbols of the Orixá who has called them during that time. They are given a new name and put in isolation which may take three weeks or more. During isolation, important information regarding the Orixá is passed on, like sacrifices they will accept and rules they should observe. After this period ends, their head is shaved, a sacrifice is made, and markings may be made to parts of their body. They are reintroduced to the community in a "coming out" ceremony. They return home where they may begin their journey in serving their Orixá. The initiate may return for a more extended apprenticeship at the temple to gain more knowledge and climb up the ranks, taking years. When they have gone through this process, they are now a priest.

Another essential part of Candomblé is divination. For example, Ifá divination. The Yoruba god of divination and knowledge is Orunmila, who also goes by Ifá. Ifá priests and priestesses are responsible for initiating new Ifá diviners and practicing Ifá divination. Orunmila is thought to be responsible for dispensing knowledge among the gods and people. Ifá is practiced by casting a divination chain on a mat or sixteen palm nuts on a divination tray. The casting results in one of the possible 256 Signs of Ifá or Signatures of Ifá. Then, the diviner will trace a pattern using their fingers over the powder covering the nuts. The divinator will then offer an interpretation and a solution to the client. Ifá training or apprenticeship can take decades. Ifá diviners are called babaloa in Yoruba traditions and Bokonon in Fon and Ewe traditions.

The second last type of Candomblé priest is the Ossayin priest, an expert herbalist. Their expertise comes from knowing how various herbs can be used in rituals to heal and so much more. They are venerators of the Orixá Ossayin, an Orixá of healing herbs. Lastly, we have babaojé which are Egungun priests dedicated to worshiping ancestors as a collective (not just one). Some of those venerated in the group is understood to have been part of the Candomblé community and served it well. They are ancestors of all Afro-Brazilians, and they are honored for their continued support and work within the community. Ancestor worship does not happen in Candomblé temples where the Orixá are worshiped. Instead, they have their own separate houses of worship. Only men can be initiated into the position of babaojé. But, there are other roles that women may assume in the Egungun houses, like lalodé, who is responsible for the group of women in the house.

SEVEN

Egungun Festival

ONE OF THE THINGS THAT MANY AFRICAN TRIBES BELIEVE IN IS ancestors. When a relative dies, they don't go to another place where they never contact us until the day we die and join them. They become guardians of the family or, if they are displeased, they harass the family or family members. Believing in ancestors as being active among the living goes against typical Christian/Western ideas about the nature of the world and death. There is a stark metaphysical difference between the two. Still, thanks to colonization, that difference has been watered down and made almost irrelevant. Despite that, it is still there. These developments, even in the western world, are relatively new.

Multiple competing philosophical ideas about how the world is really like exist. But the ones of the most interest to us are dualism and monism. In duality, the assertion is that two essential things in the world are different: material things and immaterial things. Christianity might not have started with such strong ideas about the world. Still, developments in the 17th Century influenced western religious thought.

Material things extend in space and are physical, made up of atoms, energy, and such. They are like chairs, your body, and anything you can interact with your senses. Immaterial things do not exist in space and are not physical like spirits, thoughts, and the color green (a mental perception). Now, if material and immaterial things are fundamentally different, there is no way they could interact. Items that have causal relationships are the same in some way. But because we see non-material things (like thoughts) cause physical things to happen (like typing out these words), we have to conclude that they are the same in some way. Therefore, there cannot exist two fundamentally different things that make up existence. That is one of the significant problems of dualism and why some people believe in monism. Monism believes that all of existence is made of the same basic stuff, although it might look and act very differently.

Christians believe that if people die, they cross over to the next life, a purely spiritual world. Between this world and the next one, there is a clear separation. Interestingly, angels and other agents of God or the devil may still act in the world to influence it, despite them being spiritual. In this view, being spiritual is purely immaterial, and the world is material. So, when our loved ones die, we generally think of them as gone or having taken a different shape.

In traditional African ideas, spiritual and material things are not fundamentally different. Sure, we can't see spiritual things just as readily as we see the material world, but they exist among us in the world and beyond. To Africans, the physical world is a kind of shadow—a cover—of the spiritual world (the real world), not a totally different substance from the other. As vast as it is, the universe is just a shadow of the true splendor of the world beneath.

So, when a person dies, they shed their physical skin and step into the actual/real world underneath. As a result, they are often referred to as the "living dead." If they want, the dead can be far from us and continue their journey, but they can also visit and stick around. They are, in many ways, a part of the community. It's not that the spiritual world is boring, and there is nothing to do. It is believed to be even more vibrant but still a part of this world in many ways.

When ancestors are called, they can come and assist us using their newfound powers and insight. They can observe things we can't; therefore, they know what's best. The power of the ancestors comes from the gods, and they are direct servants of the gods. They are given freedom and permission to take charge of specific communities like business or the arts.

You will find many discussions online suggesting a dualist picture of Candomblé because of colonialism or cross-pollination of ideas. For instance, people will talk about how making sacrifices to Exú opens a connection or a gateway to the spiritual world. This is somewhat different from what West African spirituality, from which Candomblé is based, thinks is happening (although you still find similar languages). However, it is not a big difference because the belief in ancestors is very close to ideas that the spiritual and physical world exist next to each other.

This brings us to Egungun, a masquerade held by African religions to venerate the ancestors (the word also refers to ancestral worship, especially in South America). In this ceremony, ancestors are invited to temporarily possess trained community members and speak to the community to uphold their values. Ancestors can bless the community and speak to the issues facing the community. Sometimes the spirits may even give particular messages to individuals. The devotees invite the spirits to possess them to wear masks, elaborate customs, and dance to drums until ancestors possess them.

The primary Egungun festival occurs in June when community members come to the marketplace and perform masked dances. The masks they put on represent ancestral spirits and may encompass the whole body or just the face.

The maskers all dance together; although each possesses his own drum accompaniment and an entourage of chorusing women and girls. The festivities climax with the arrival of Andu, the highly dynamic mask. It is thought that the departed souls possess the maskers while they are dancing. Although it encourages a sense of individuality between the living and the dead, the festival also triggers a certain measure of fear. There aren't any big Egungun events in Brazil as those you see in West African countries, but Candomblé followers still build shrines to ancestors and make offerings. In Brazil, Egungun ceremonies are performed in separate houses to the temples of the Orixás. The dead can visit their offspring through these connections. It is worth noting that Egungun is also a word describing a collection of ancestors rather than one.

EIGHT

Candomblé Religious Festivals

Senhor dos Navegantes Festival

THERE IS NOTHING QUITE LIKE SENHOR DOS NAVEGANTES Festival on New Year's Eve and New Year's Day. Candomblé has millions of followers in South America. It is a religion that has plenty of celebrations and rituals to keep adherents united. Salvador is where the religion came about. Senhor dos Navegantes Festival on New Year's Eve and New Year's Day are known for their beautiful celebrations. There are decorated boats that pay homage to all the saints. In addition to this, music and samba processions make the event truly memorable.

Filled with Life

Most Candomblé followers dress up in white robes and gather around altars while holding gardenias. As the processions commerce, members fall into a trance and writhe to the music. They let out loud, intense screams. The festivities are filled with life. Anyone who attends would tell you that the experience is unlike anything they have witnessed in their lives. You will be amazed by the variety of colors that make up the festival. The African-based religion is steeped in rituals, and adherents hope to get possessed by the spirit of the God of Fire, Xangô. Comprising both African paganism and Portuguese Catholicism, enslaved West Africans brought the traditions to the New World.

The religion has an uninhibited sense that you will notice in its followers. The enslaved Africans who had arrived bringing with them their pantheon of gods who personified forces like water, wind, and fire. Their allegiance to the animate and inanimate, such as food, days of the week, colors, and animals, is what makes them unique.

Etiquette Tips for Senhor dos Navegantes Festival on New Year's Eve and New Year's Day

You will need to know about specific etiquette tips if you observe the Candomblé festival or ceremony. Although there might be many places of worship, you will need to head over to the dodgier parts of the city to get a glimpse into the culture.

Keep away from wearing skimpy outfits and dress appropriately. Generally, it is advised that people wear white clothing.

During the ceremonies, no photos or videos can be taken. Visitors can only observe. Therefore, you should not expect to participate. Follow what the crowd does. If people are standing, you should also stand.

Before you decide to eat any ceremonial food or partake in the dancing, you must understand that the practices are only reserved for adherents. There is no admission price for entering a place of worship. However, you can make a donation to the spiritual leader.

Now that you know more about Senhor dos Navegantes Festival on New Year's Eve and New Year's Day, you can attend the festival and experience the West African religion firsthand. Make sure to show respect and do what others do.

The Washing of Bonfim

The washing of Bonfim staircases is a popular celebration on the second Thursday of January every year. It is one of the most extensive manifestations of Bahia. Thousands of adherents gather to participate in the event. It is a spiritual walk typically held in Lower City, Salvador. It is held between the Sacred Hill in Bonfim and the Church of Our Lady.

As the event is unlike any other, it is definitely worth attending. It offers an unforgettable experience. In its essence, the event is all about dedication and surrender for the greater good. The celebration is marked by a boat trip, a scared run, and religious syncretism. The Sacred Hill area has been completely restored. A beautiful party marks the day.

Faith

The washing of Bonfim starts at the Church of Our Lady. A worship service is offered early in the morning. The processions are held in unison until adherents reach the Church of Bonfim. All types of devotees come together during the event. Then, they walk towards the Church of Our Lord of Bonfim, which is at a distance of 8km. The journey is marked by various processions. Once the worship service is completed, devotees start their journey. Upon their arrival at the Sacred Hill, the staircase is where. There is also a feast that has been hosted for over two centuries. It brings members and tourists together.

Sacred Running

For over three decades, the Sacred Running has been held. The Lower City is filled with energy as participants run at full speed. The run starts from the Church of Our Lady. It is up to you to either sign up to go in a group or on your own. The gyms that dot the city also have their own private groups. Considered the liveliest street race in the country, it is a tradition for residents to participate in the running.

The Walk

The walk starts from the Church of Our Lady. It is a sightseeing tour of the city. The journey includes two postcards: the Elevator of the Upper City and Model Market, home to over 300 stores that sell local souvenirs and handicrafts. It goes through different neighborhoods. There are many food stalls where you can eat all types of food and music is played by locals. The coffee carts also use speakers to play folklore and get creative. Closed parties are also held to celebrate the moment. The music helps put people at ease and makes their journey much lighter.

Now that you know everything about the washing of Bonfim on the secondary Thursday of January, you can participate in it to get a sense of the local culture. The people's beliefs and traditions make your time in Salvador worth it. Besides, the locals will accept you with open arms and help you better understand the different festivities.

Festivals of Yemanja

When the second month of the year rolls around, Brazilians across the country, regardless of their faith, celebrate Yemanja, the goddess of the sea. Things are even bigger in the city of Salvador. The festivities tend to be huge and attract massive crowds. The Rio Vermelho neighborhood is where the celebration is the largest. Every February 2nd is a fantastic time as Candomblé adherents offer gifts and flowers to the goddess towards the edge of the sea and send them into the ocean. Everyone has to wear white clothing to mark the occasion. There is also lots of music and dancing involved.

The Iemanjá festival, called Yemoja in Nigeria, is the most significant major celebration in Candomblé and related African religions. Here we will look at the African and Brazilian iteration of the Iemanjá festival.

As we have established, Iemanjá is considered the mother of almost all gods. She is associated with water bodies for a variety of reasons, one of which is that water gives life and is essential to life. So, she is associated with rejuvenation, prosperity, good health, and maternity. However, she represents very different things to different people. Iemanjá is celebrated annually in big festivals. No matter when they occur, these celebrations mark the beginning of a new year and new blessings for believers. In Nigeria, the festival is called Yemoja Festival, and in Brazil, it is widely known as the Yemanja festival.

Yemoja Festival - Nigeria

Yemoja festival is the Yoruba version, which is believed not to have changed for hundreds of years. The festival takes place in October over 17 days, ending on the last day of the month with a final procession to the nearest river, where offerings are made to Yemoja and the spirits that reside in the water.

Increasingly newer people joining in the celebrations nowadays do so because they want to rediscover their African identity outside of the domination of Islam and Christianity. On the final day, followers gather at the Yemoja Temple, where her 400-year-old statue resides. They offer thanks to the goddess for their continued wellness. People speak their prayer to kola nuts which are then put in a hollowed calabash with other offerings like corn, beans, fruits, and yam porridge. Then, there is a procession to the river where a chosen woman, called efunleye, carries the calabashes to the river. The contents of the calabashes are offered to Yemoja, including a pigeon's head. On this day, new initiates are shaved and wear beads that symbolize their patron Orixá.

Yemoja is thanked for the year, and if she is pleased, they will have another good year. When prayers are finished and it's time to go back, followers and priestesses gather the water in bottles to be used in healing baths, medicine, and other rituals. The water is believed to be empowered to rejuvenate and bless. The head priestess may sprinkle it on gathering devotees to bless them.

Yemanja Festival - Brazil

It is the Candomblé version of the Yemoja festival. In Salvador, the festival is celebrated on the 2nd of February. In Rio de Janeiro, it happens on the 1st of January. The celebrations in Rio de Janeiro begin on the 31st of December when followers and the general public gather at the beach. At this time, altars are made from candles planted in the sand, and within the outline, flowers, letters, and fruits are put up as offerings.

Others put their offerings on miniature boats along with tiny representations of the things they wish Yemanja to bless them with, like motorbikes, houses, or cars. There are other typical offerings in these boats like fruits, flowers, perfume, lipstick, and more. As the clock hits midnight, these boats are pushed off the shore to sail into the sea to where Yemonja resides. Others may throw flowers and other offerings into the sea. There is praying, singing, music, fireworks, and firecrackers during this time.

Shortly after, the whole affair turns into a New Year's Eve party. The celebration continues until dawn. The philosophical underpinnings of this tradition are the same as the Yoruba's, which is thanking the goddess and praying for a better year.

The biggest celebration of Yemanja occurs in Salvador on the 2nd of February. Like Rio de Janeiro, it is often broadcast on TV. The festivities start at sunrise with fireworks when followers gather at Rio Vermelho. Offerings are made to the shrines around the beach. Around 4 p.m., fishermen load their boats with offerings and sail out to sea to offer them to the Yemanja.

There is nothing quite like the Festival of Yemanja. Anyone who visits the festival is welcomed and can expect to have a great time.

National Day of the Samba

When December rolls around, National Samba Day is held in Brazil to celebrate everything in life. In addition to its stunning landscapes, Brazil offers samba. It is a style of music that highlights the diversity of the nation. The Day of the Samba revolves around the Brazilian identity, all about keeping traditions alive, including musical style.

Initially, the residents of Salvador de Bahia used to celebrate Samba Day. As its popularity spread throughout the country, it became a national event. As Brazilians are highly talented, samba reflects the country's vitality, love, and traditions. Despite various musical styles, samba is considered the most beautiful as it reflects the personality of the Brazilian people.

The celebrations start on December 1st and last until December 2nd. The musical rhythm is celebrated on the Day of the Samba. It allows people from different regions to come together. People from across the globe know that the samba represents Brazil. Despite samba being famous in every part of Brazil, it is associated with Sao Paulo, Bahia, and Rio de

Janeiro. The dance was performed by enslaved people who added their regional rhythms.

Origins

December 2nd has been selected as the Day of the Samba because during this very day, Ary Barroso, the famous composer, visited Salvador da Bahia and brought the culture to the world. Samba Day was proposed in his honor by Luis Monteiro Costa, the former city councilor. Over time, the festival has become a part of the national identity.

Modern Samba

During the 1950s, the samba schools decided to hold a bourgeois carnival in Rio de Janeiro. What followed led to the most significant public festival in the world. The samba schools have the ultimate parade comprising hundreds of dancers and musicians. The event characterizes the samba and is broadcasted nationwide. A theme is performed by each samba school.

Wind instruments are played, which had been previously prohibited. There is also lots of singing and groups that enter the parade. The Cavaquinho is a melodic instrument that is widely used to highlight the entrance of each group. Thousands of spectators get to watch the beauty of the music and dance. Modern samba combines the faces of Brazil to offer something completely unique. Sao Paulo and Rio de Janeiro host the event with full enthusiasm. However, other cities also host the event. The instruments have been tuned higher over time, and the samba is performed even more quickly. Anyone who visits Rio de Janeiro must consider attending the Day of the Samba.

For those who are lucky, the Day of the Samba is a spectacular event that you need to attend at least once in your lifetime. It is filled with passion and love. Everyone is in a good mood and ready to minge. It also provides the perfect opportunity for you to meet the locals and have some fun.

Santa Barbara

Santa Barbara is a popular holiday in Brazil. Although it is not an official holiday, thousands of people commemorate the saint every year on December 4th. It is a day of the feast. There is a legend about the saint who was considered to possess great beauty. Her father, a pagan, had locked her up in a tower to prevent suitors from pursuing her. He also grew tired of her habit of helping the poor who were followers of Christianity, a new religion at that time. His fear of his daughter converting to Christianity took root, and Saint Barbara ended up professing her love for the new religion. This led to him executing her and lighting striking him as a result thereof. Although Santa Barbara is celebrated in unison across the globe, it is observed differently in Brazil due to the influences of West African religions.

How Is Santa Barbara Celebrated?

The celebrations of Santa Barbara start early on December 4th. A religious service is held. Catholicism is mixed with Candomblé and Umbanda in Salvador. Thus, everyone is welcome to participate in the ceremony. Each saint is included by the religion, which makes it inclusive. As Santa Barbara is a more significant festival, everyone is fully embraced. After the religious service is completed, a short procession is held at the city square and essential neighborhoods. Offerings are made for a safe year.

There is plenty of food and drinks offered to everyone after the procession is complete. It includes traditional Candomblé foods like caruru, lensa, and more. As the religious part of the festival comes to an end by mid-day, the historic center comes to life with parties that last until the night. There are also artistic programs during the afternoon, and everyone is in full enthusiasm. Stages are set up all over the cities. Music is blasted into the night as the festivities keep everyone going. There are also samba and reggae performances. They are widely popular, and other styles are represented at the event. Everyone is free to participate in the event as it is open to the public. Hence, you can wander as you please without dealing with any sort of restrictions.

Tips for Attending Santa Barbara

If you decide to attend Santa Barbara, you need to consider the following information for your enjoyment as well as safety.

First, wear white and red. As white and red are the traditional colors of the followers of Candomblé, you have to wear either of the two to attend the festival.

You should plan for the crowds. Understandable, as many as 10,000 people attend the religious part of the event. Hence, you must prepare for the crowds. With the large crowd, watch your belongings. With countless people attending, drinking, having fun, and conversing, there are likely to be pickpockets. Thus, you must carefully hold onto your money, phone, and keys.

Now that you know what to expect from Santa Barbara, you can finally attend the event and have the time of your life.

Our Lady of Conceicao du Praia

The religion of Candomblé is unique. It is an amalgamation of West African religion and Catholicism. Various festivals are held by adherents of the unique religion. One of the festivals you might have heard of is Our Lady of Conceicao du Praia on December 8th. It is held at the Basilica of Our Lady of

Conceicao du Praia. The festival honors the Unique Patroness and Excellence of Bahia. As the oldest religious festival in the country, followers have shown devotion and faith in the Immaculate Conceicao for close to five centuries. The festival's theme is to celebrate Our Lady of Conceicao du Praia.

A trio that has been elected from the Basilica's choir are followed by seminaries, priests, faithful, and the population. Tribute is given to Our Lady of Conceicao du Praia. She is adored by the followers of Candomblé and Catholics alike. The saint is considered to be the goddess of freshwaters by the former. At 5am, the preparations start. However, the Eucharistic Celebration takes place at 9am in the morning. You will need to visit at 8am for the best seat inside the Basilica. It is held by the Most Reverend, Archbishop of Salvador da Bahia. There is also music that is accompanied by the choir that is performed by Maestro David Alves. The church is about holding onto musical tradition, and the songs are excellent.

The Solemn Eucharistic Celebration starts at 9am and continues until 10.30am when the procession is left by Conceicao da Praia. It covers Miguel Calmon Street, Da Franca Avenue, Holanda Street, and goes back to Belgica Steet. It also includes Lafayette Coutinho before moving back to the Basilica. The Blessed Sacrament Solemn processions are held by the afternoon, followed by the priests commemorating.

Conclusion

African religions are rich and complex in a way that I don't think a book can truly capture. The natural beauty of it all is captured by experiencing it yourself and immersing yourself in the culture. I hope this book has sparked an interest in you to go and explore. There are bound to be plenty of surprises out there.

So, what are the core lessons of this book?

The first one is that Candomblé is based on African traditions and philosophies of hundreds of years old. It is a religion born out of displacement and a need to reconnect. Religion is shaped by a confluence of factors, not because it wanted to, but because of necessity.

We have learned that the creator God of Candomblé is a deist, and all the deities under them are in charge of everything else. We saw the types of philosophical problems it solves when explaining evil and appreciated the moral ambiguity or Candomblé.

We learned that people are born under the supervision and protection of an Orixá or many Orixás. This explains their temperament, personality, and their destiny in life. Orixás demand some prayers and sacrifice from followers but expect complete devotion from those who have a calling. Those who have a calling answer it by being initiated into one of the many types of priesthood. Ancestors are a part of that picture too. And we saw how African religion's view of death implies a monist interpretation of reality. We saw how these dead spirits remain a part of the community. We closed off with a brief chapter on priesthood and Candomblé celebrations to give you a taste of how things work apart from theology and philosophy.

This is by no means everything. The best lessons are learned out there, in person.

If you enjoyed this, check out the rest of the series at mojosiedlak.com/african-spirituality-and-tradition.

References

BBC. (2009 September 15). Religions. https://www.bbc.-co.uk/religion/religions/Candomblé/history/history.shtml

Encyclopedia.com. (2018). Candomblé. In Encyclopedia.com. https://www.encyclopedia.com/philosophy-and-religion/bible/early-christianity-biographies/Candomblé

Grimond, G. (2017 July 4). Brazil's Goddess of the Sea: Everything You Need to Know About Festival of Iemanjá. Culture Trip. https://theculturetrip.com/south-america/brazil/articles/brazils-goddess-of-the-sea-everything-you-need-to-know-about-festival-of-iemanja/

Herbstein, M. (n.d.). African religion and Candomblé. Ama, A Story of the Atlantic Slave Trade. Retrieved January 18, 2022, from http://www.ama.africatoday.com/Candomblé.htm

Meyer, A. (2014). Brazil Religion. Brazil. https://www.brazil.org.za/religion.html

References

Omari-Tunkara, M. S. (2005). Manipulating the sacred: Yorùbá art, ritual, and resistance in Brazilian Candomblé. Wayne State University Press.

Asante, M. K., & Mazama, A. (2008). Encyclopedia of African religion. Sage Publications.

Poppino, R. E., & Schneider, R. M. (2019). History of Brazil. In Encyclopedia Britannica. https://www.britannica.com/place/Brazil/History

Shahbandeh, M. (2021 May 21). Sugar industry - statistics & facts. Statista. https://www.statista.com/topics/1224/sugar/

About the Author

Monique Joiner Siedlak is a writer, witch, and warrior on a mission to awaken people to their greatest potential through the power of storytelling infused with mysticism, modern paganism, and new age spirituality. At the young age of 12, she began rigorously studying the fascinating philosophy of Wicca. By the time she was 20, she was self-initiated into the craft, and hasn't looked back ever since. To this day, she has authored over 50 books pertaining to the magick and mysteries of life.

To find out more about Monique Joiner Siedlak artistically, spiritually, and personally, feel free to visit her **official website**.

www.mojosiedlak.com

facebook.com/mojosiedlak

twitter.com/mojosiedlak

instagram.com/mojosiedlak

pinterest.com/mojosiedlak

bookbub.com/authors/monique-joiner-siedlak

More Books by Monique

Practical Magick

Wiccan Basics

Candle Magick

Wiccan Spells

Love Spells

Abundance Spells

Herb Magick

Moon Magick

Creating Your Own Spells

Gypsy Magic

Protection Magick

Celtic Magick

Shamanic Magick

Crystal Magic

Divination Magic for Beginners

Divination with Runes: A Beginner's Guide to Rune Casting

Divination with Diloggún: A Beginner's Guide to Diloggún and Obi

Spiritual Growth and Personal Development

Creative Visualization

Astral Projection for Beginners

Meditation for Beginners

Reiki for Beginners

Manifesting With the Law of Attraction

Being an Empath Today

Communicating with Your Spirit Guides

Healing Your Inner Child: A Guide into Shadow Work

Get a Handle on Life

Stress Management

Get a Handle on Anxiety

Get a Handle on Depression

Get a Handle on Procrastination

The Yoga Collective

Yoga for Beginners

Yoga for Stress

Yoga for Back Pain

Yoga for Weight Loss

Yoga for Flexibility

Yoga for Advanced Beginners

Yoga for Fitness

Yoga for Runners

Yoga for Energy

Yoga for Your Sex Life

Yoga to Beat Depression and Anxiety

Yoga for Menstruation

Yoga to Detox Your Body

Yoga to Tone Your Body

A Natural Beautiful You

Creating Your Own Body Butter

Creating Your Own Body Scrub

Creating Your Own Body Spray

THANK YOU FOR READING MY BOOK! I REALLY APPRECIATE ALL OF YOUR FEEDBACK AND I LOVE TO HEAR WHAT YOU HAVE TO SAY. PLEASE LEAVE YOUR REVIEW AT YOUR FAVORITE RETAILER!

www.ingramcontent.com/pod-product-compliance
Lightning Source LLC
Chambersburg PA
CBHW060417050426
42449CB00009B/1997